THE LEADER WHO GAVE INSPIRING SPEECHES

Biography of Winston Churchill
Children's Biography Books

BABY PROFESSOR
EDUCATION KIDS

Speedy Publishing LLC
40 E. Main St. #1156
Newark, DE 19711
www.speedypublishing.com

Copyright © 2017

All Rights reserved. No part of this book may be reproduced or
used in any way or form or by any means whether electronic or
mechanical, this means that you cannot record or photocopy
any material ideas or tips that are provided in this book

Winston Churchill was the Prime Minister of Great Britain and was one of the great leaders of the world during the 20th century. He was born in Oxfordshire, England on November 30, 1874, and passed away in London England on January 24, 1965. Read further to learn about this man and the speeches he was known for.

BIOGRAPHY

Winston Churchill became a great world leader during the 20th century. This leadership assisted Britain to remain strong against the Germans and Hitler, even though it was the final country fighting. He also became well known for his inspiring quotes and speeches.

Sir Winston Churchill age 68, 1942

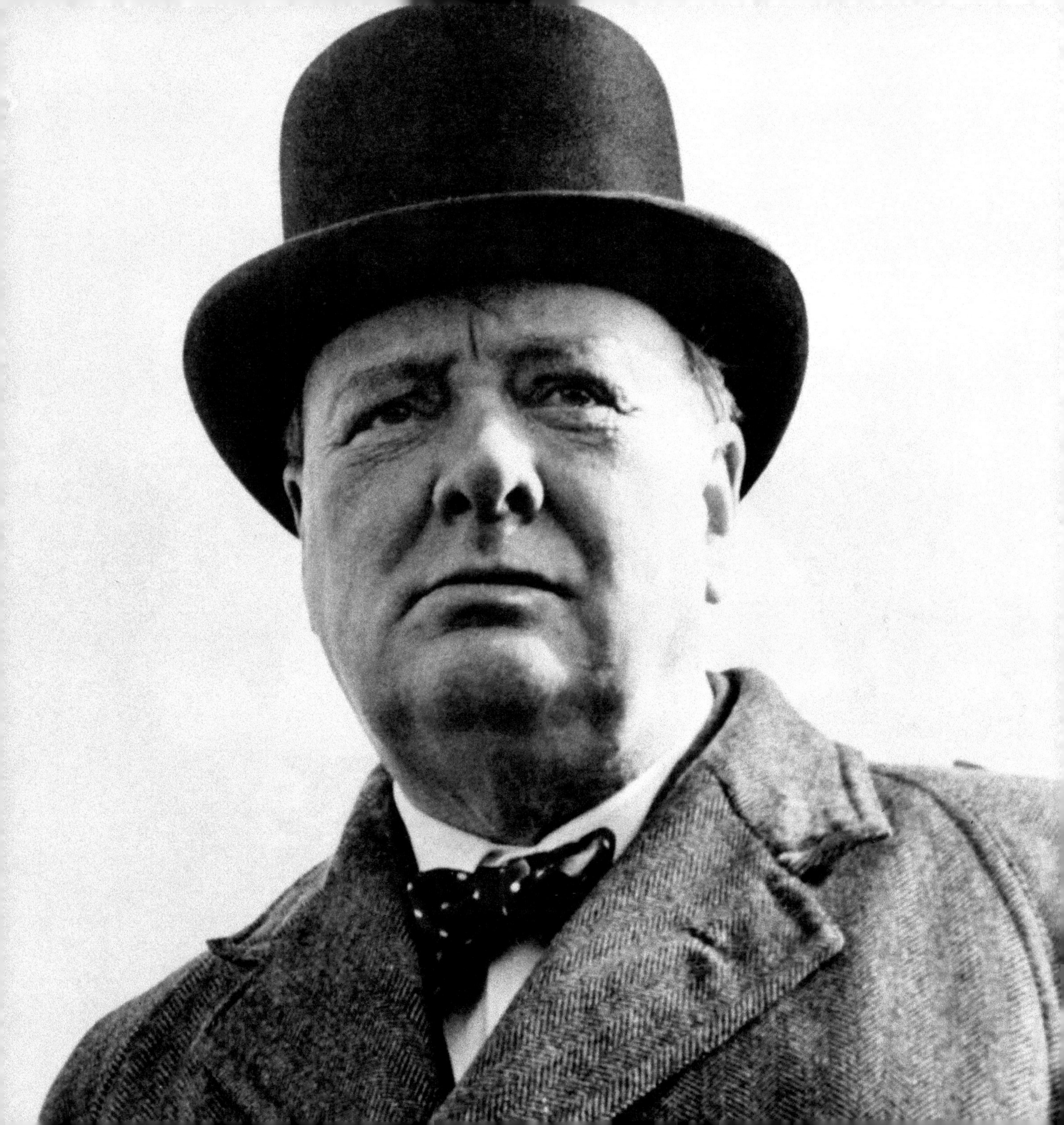

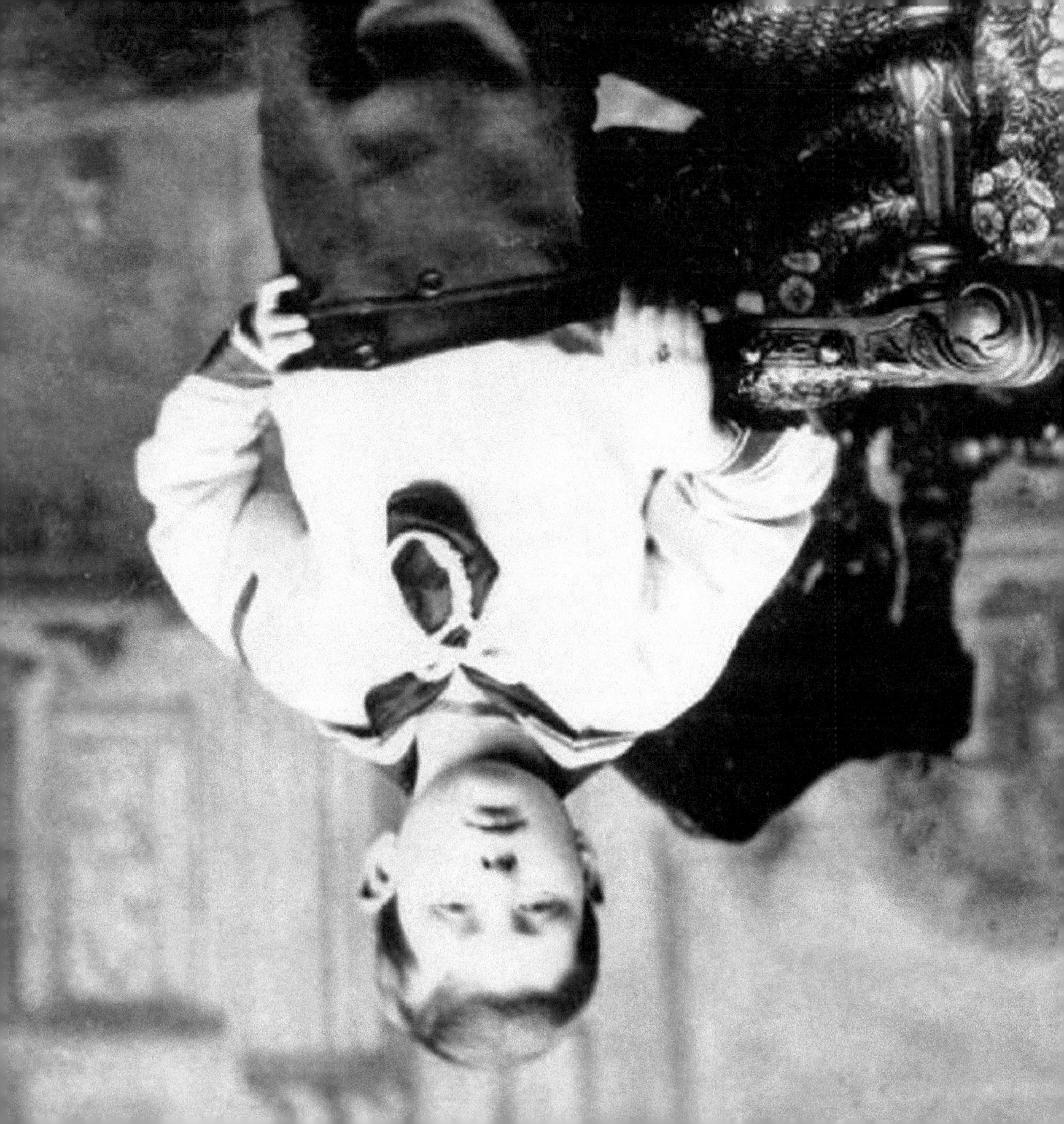

CHILDHOOD AND GROWING UP

He was born at a palace that was known as Blenheim Palace in Oxfordshire, England, on November 30, 1874, to affluent aristocrats. Lord Randolph Churchill, his father, was a politician and held many higher offices in Britain's government.

Winston Churchill aged seven, in 1881

JOINING THE MILITARY

He joined Britain's Calgary once he graduated from the Royal Military College. While serving with the military he traveled to faraway places working as a newspaper correspondent, writing about battles and life in the military.

Winston Churchill in military uniform, 1895

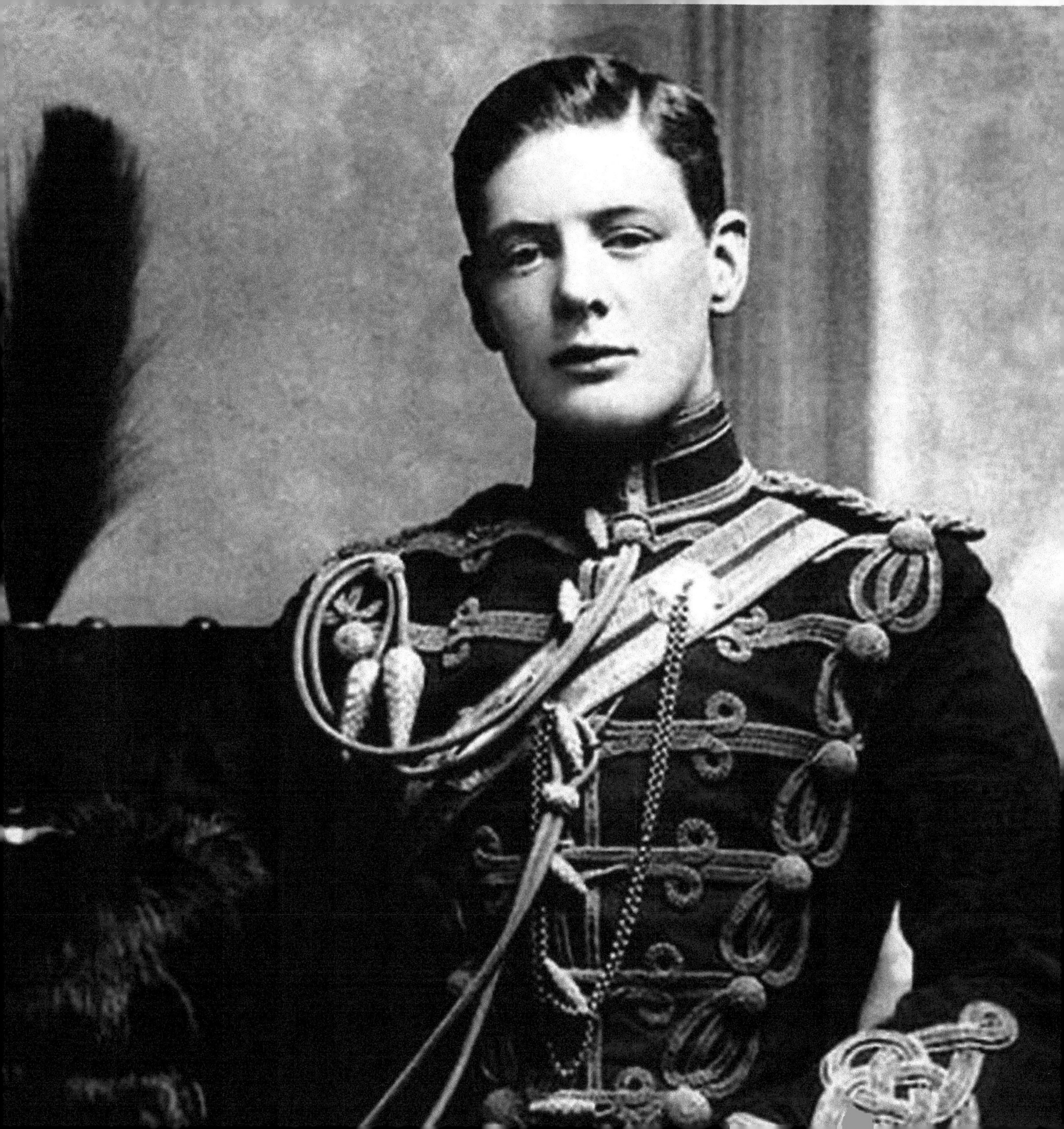

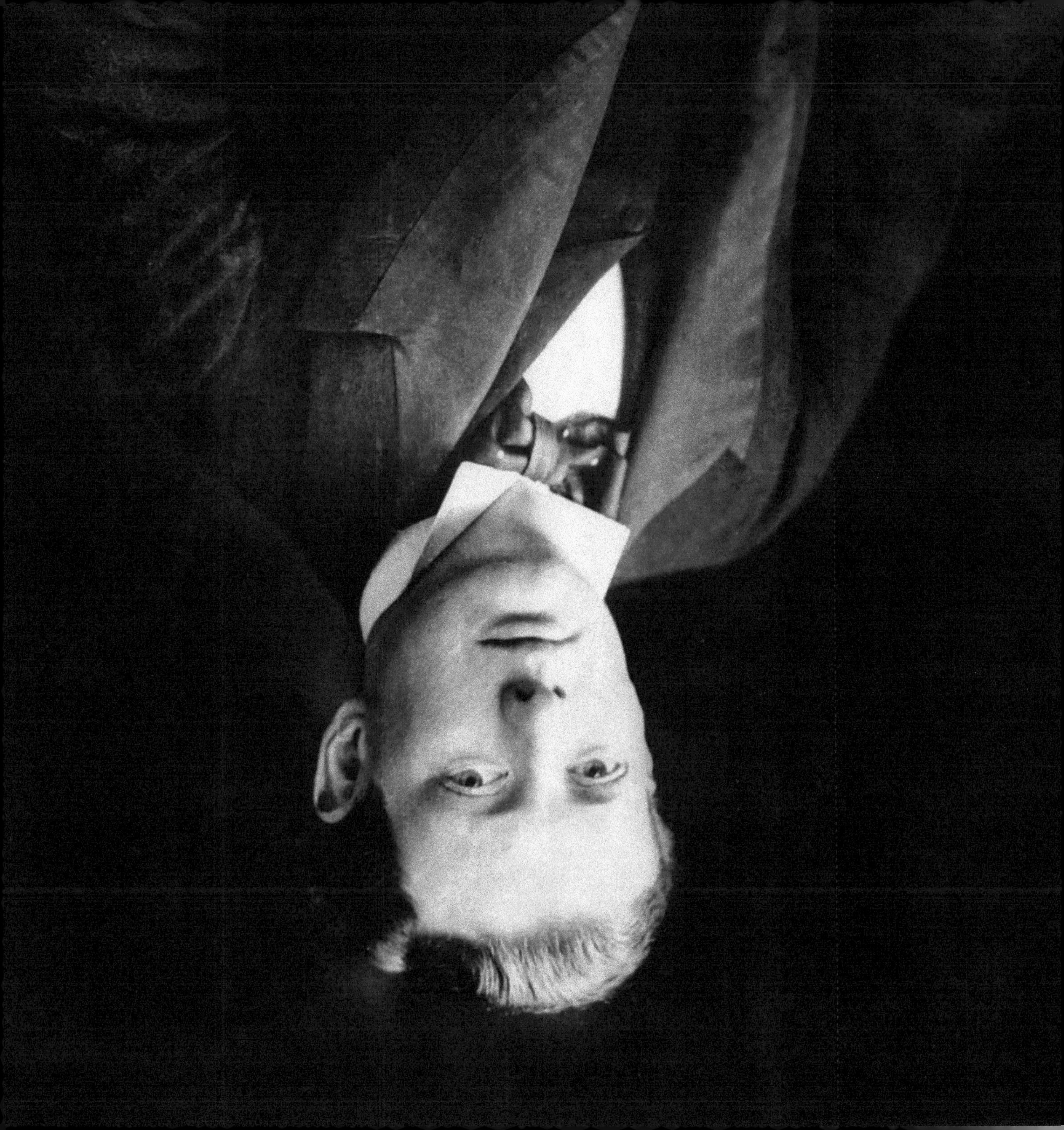

While serving in the Second Boer War in South Africa, he became a prisoner of war after being captured. He was then able to escape and traveled for 300 miles in order to be rescued. He then became a hero for a while in Britain.

A young Winston Churchill in 1900

RISE TO POWER

In 1900 he became elected to the Parliament. During the next 30 years, he held various positions with the government, which, in 1908, included a cabinet post. He experienced many ups and downs at this time, but also was famous for his many writings.

Winston Churchill age 26 in 1900

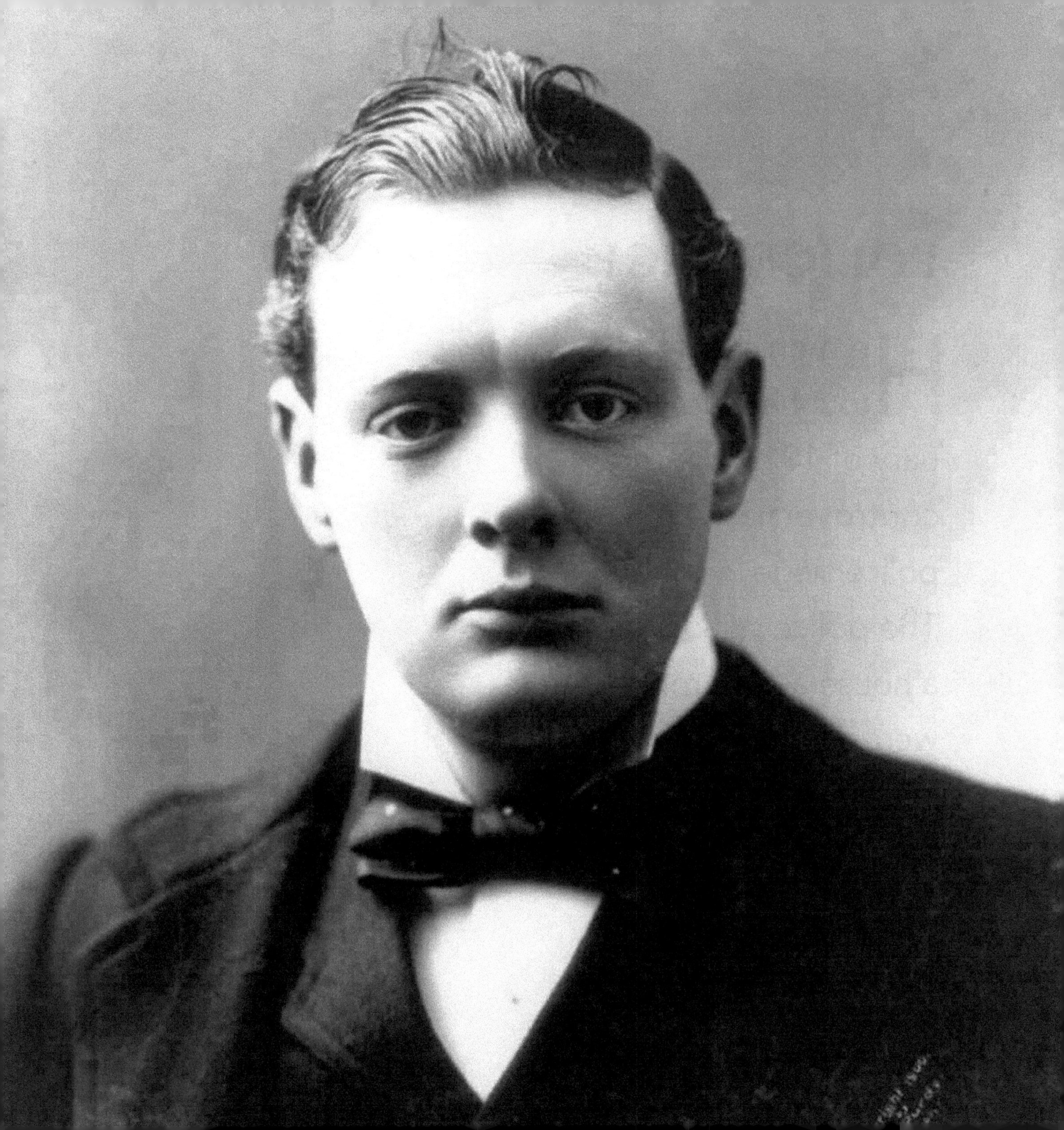

POLICE SIEGE

He then showed his tougher side in January of 1911, making a controversial visit at a police siege in London. The police surrounded a house as two robbers were caught.

Sir Winston Churchill (highlighted), at Sidney Street with Police Officer

Sir Winston Churchill

The amount of his participation in this siege remains to be disputed. Some say that he went to the scene to only see what was happening, while others say that he instructed the police as to how best to enter the building.

Winston Churchill age 30 in 1904

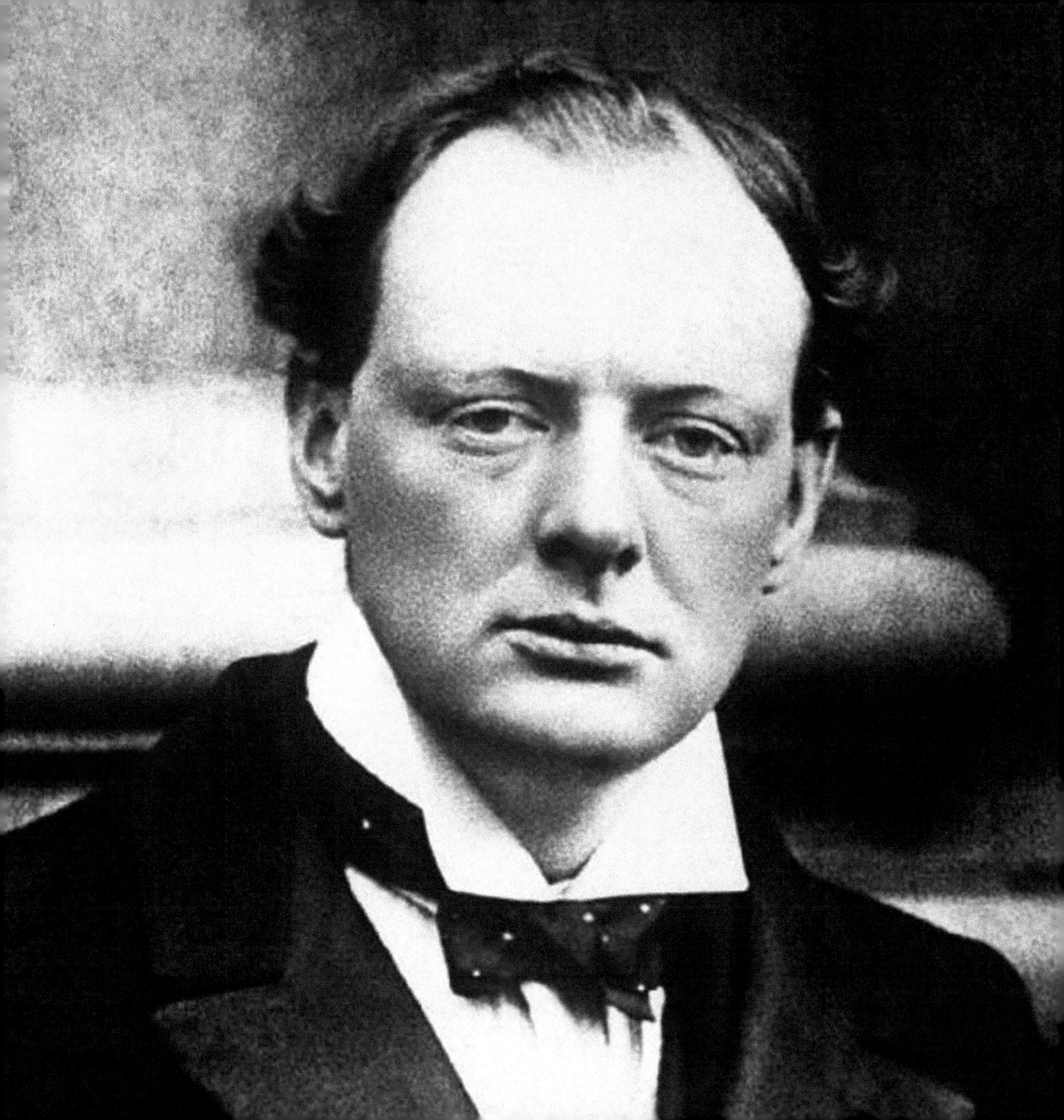

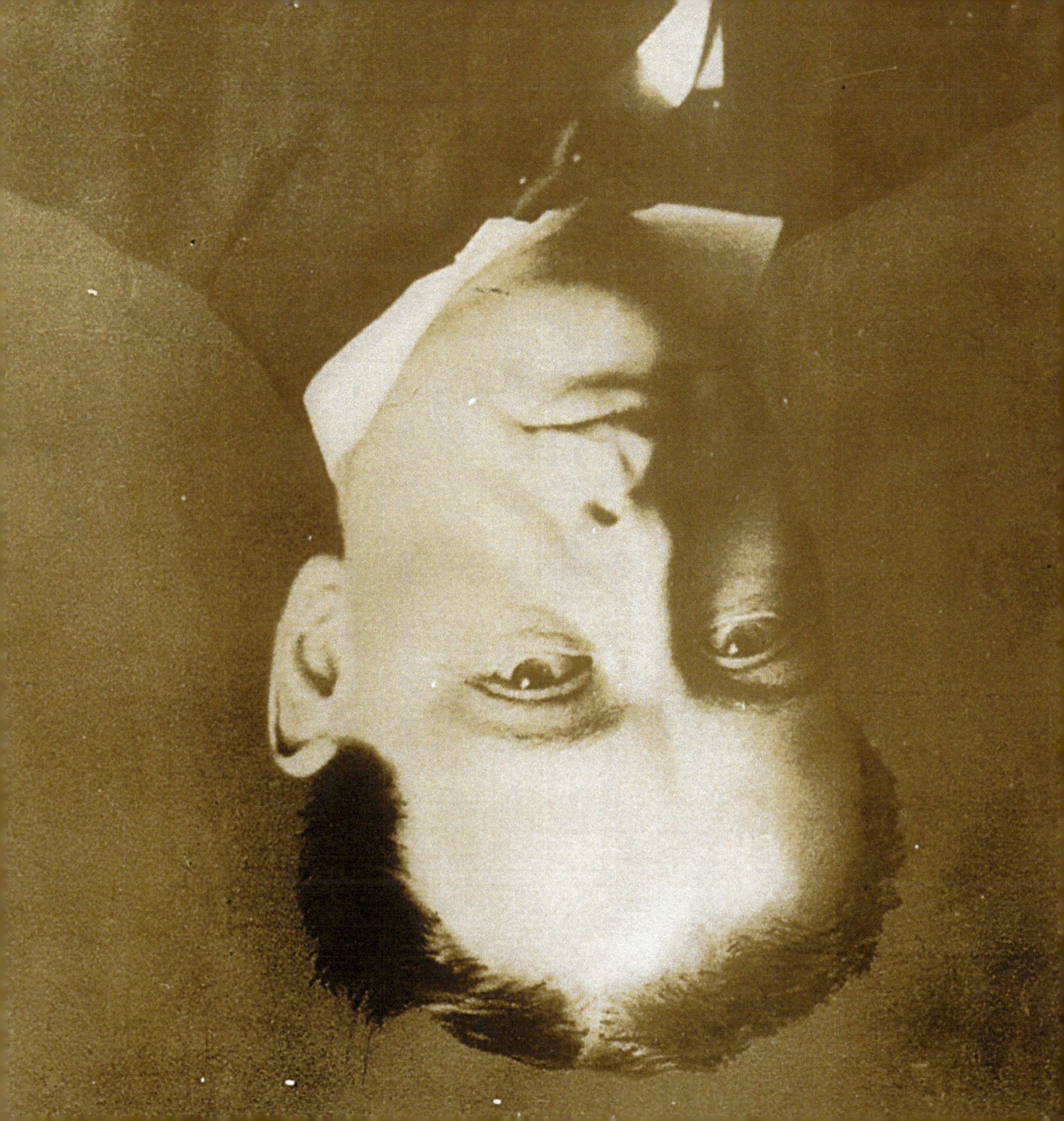

It is known that it caught on fire and he prevented the flames from being extinguished, indicated that he felt it was best to "let the house burn down" rather than risk the lives of the fire brigade in attempting to rescue the people inside. The two robbers' remains were found inside.

Winston Churchill in 1917

FAMILY

Churchill was married to Clementine Hozier in 1908, and they had five children, one son and four daughters.

Clementine Churchill in 1915

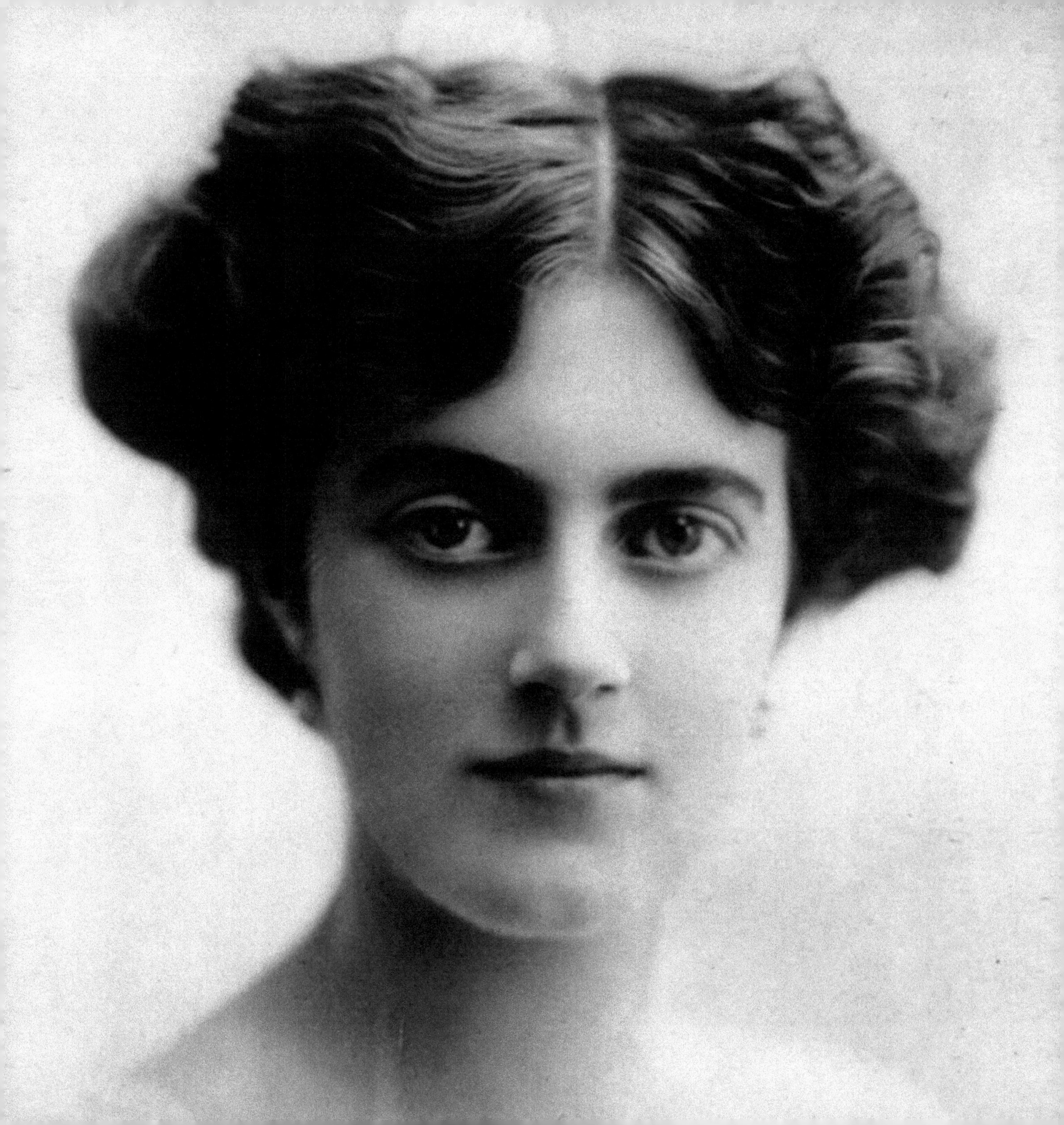

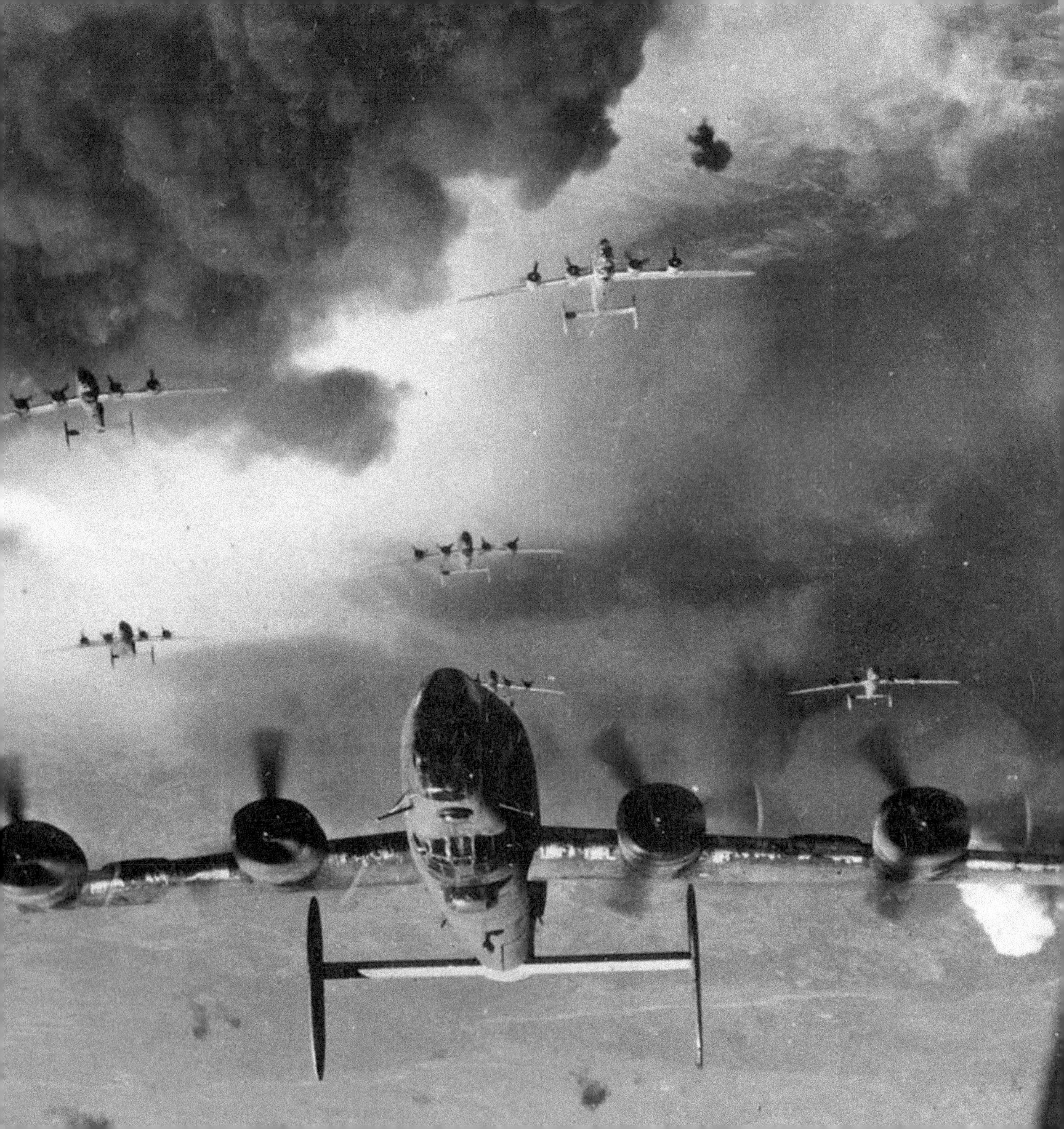

B-24D Bomber Planes fly over Polesti during World War II

WORLD WAR II

Even though he did not see Hitler's threat as he gained power in 1933, Churchill started to become an advocate for British rearmament. As Germany started to control their neighbors in 1938, he then became a staunch critic of Prime Minister Chamberlain's policy regarding appeasement of the Nazis.

On the day Britain declared war on Germany, September 3, 1939, Churchill became named first lord of the Admiralty as well as a member of its war cabinet. By April of 1940, he became the chairman of the Military Coordinating Committee. Germany then invaded and occupied Norway later that month, which became a setback for Chamberlain. Chamberlain was resisting Churchill's proposal to have Britain preempt the German attack by occupying dire Norwegian sea ports and iron mines, unilaterally.

A debate in May regarding the Norwegian crisis resulted in a no confidence vote regarding Prime Minister Chamberlain. King George VI then appointed Churchill as prime minister and the minister of defense on May 10. Within a few hours, the German Army started its Western Offensive, invading Belgium, Luxembourg, and the Netherlands. After two days, the German forces entered into France and Britain now stood alone.

British Prime Minister Winston Churchill is greeted at Gatow Airport in Berlin

Prime Minister Winston Churchill visits Caen France in 1944

He then quickly created a coalition cabinet consisting of leaders from the Conservative, Liberal, and Labor parties. He placed talented and intelligent men in major positions. He then, on June 18, 1940, made the iconic speech to the House of Commons, warning that "the Battle of Britain" was getting ready to start.

He was able to keep resistance to the Nazi dominance going, and then created the foundation for the alliance with the Soviet Union and the United States. He previously had cultivated a friendship with U.S. President Franklin Roosevelt during the 1930s, and then by March of 1941, he secured vital U.S. aid from the Lend Lease Act, which permitted Britain to be able to order war supplies on credit from the United States.

Once the United States, in December of 1941, entered into WWII, he felt confident the Allies eventually would win. Churchill then worked close with President Roosevelt and Joseph Stalin, the leader of the Soviet Union and forged the Allied strategy and the post-war life.

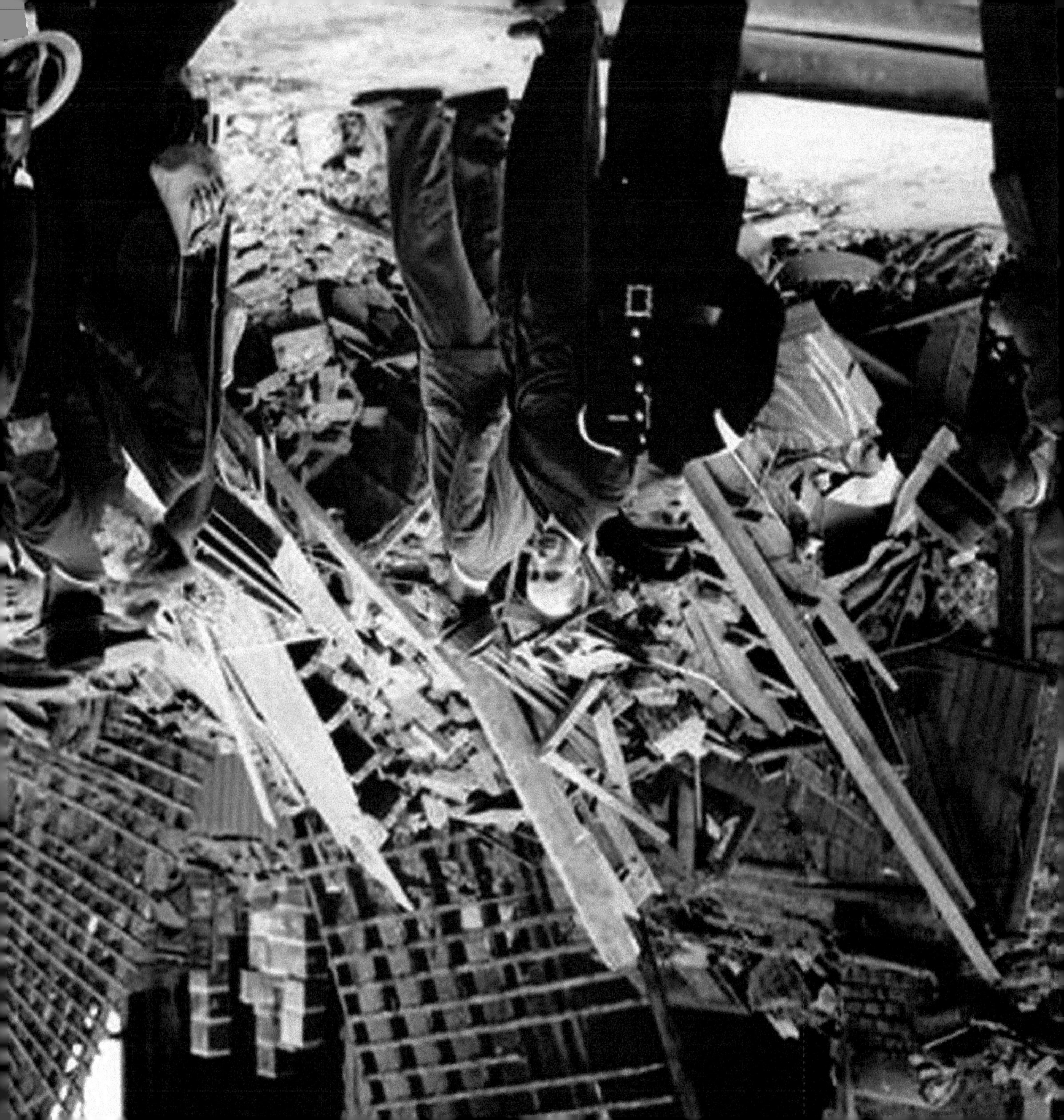

Winston Churchill visiting bomb-damaged areas of the East End of London, 1940

During meetings in Teheran in 1943, Yalta in February of 1945, and Potsdam in July of 1945, he worked with these leaders in developing a strategy against Axis Powers, and assisted with organizing the post-war world with the centerpiece being the United Nations. Churchill proposed ideas for Britain's social reforms once the war was winding down, but wasn't able to persuade the public. In July 1945, he was defeated in their general election.

He then became leader of the opposition party during the following six years, and would continue having an impact on world affairs. While visiting the United States in March of 1946, is when he made his "Iron Curtain" speech, warning of the Soviet command over Eastern Europe. He then also advocated for Britain to remain independent of the European alliances and retain their independence.

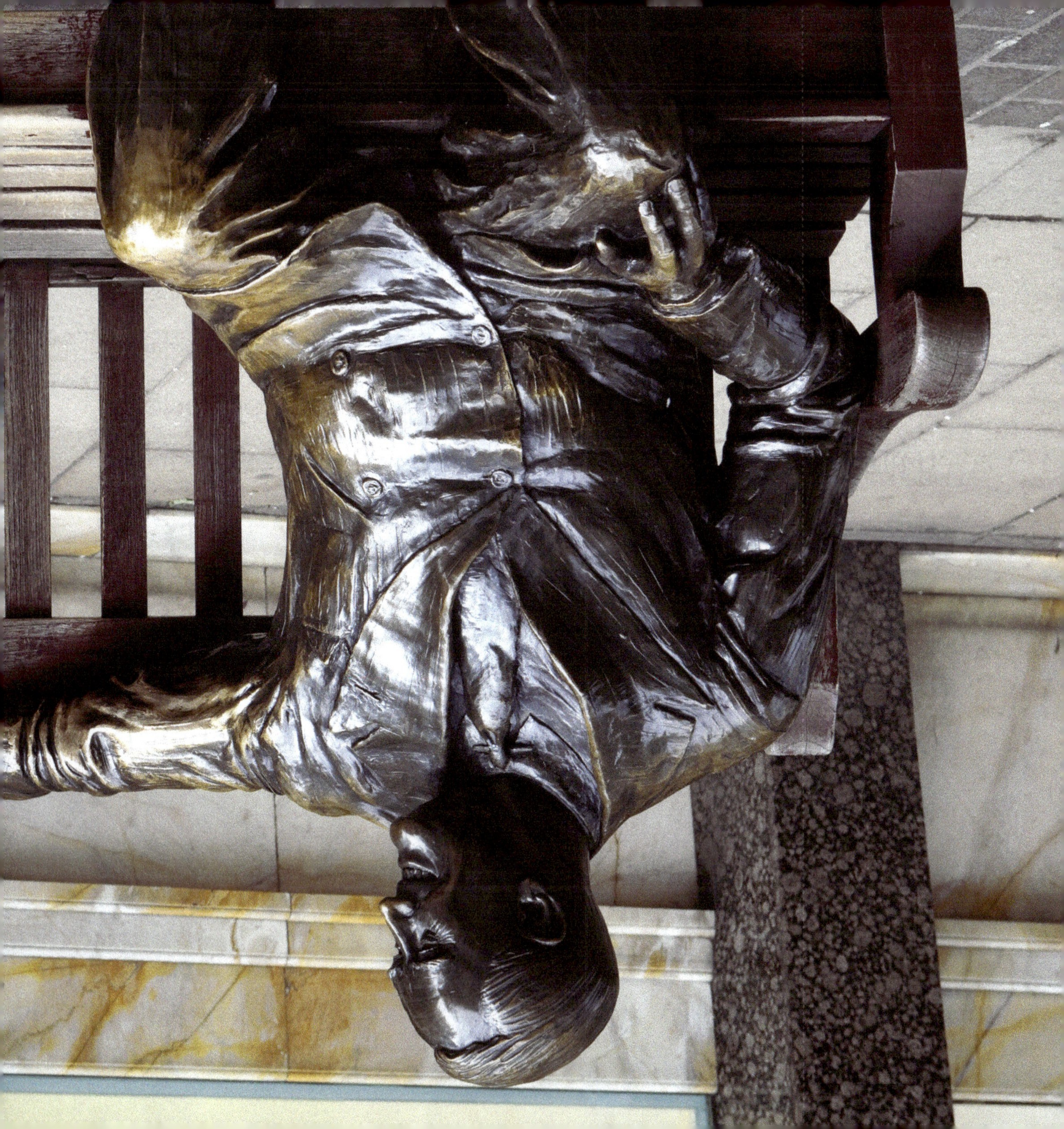

Statues of Franklin D. Roosevelt and Winston Churchill 'talking' to each other in London's Mayfair

He returned to government after the election of 1951. He became appointed as minister of defense from October 1951 through January 1952, becoming prime minister in October of 1951. Queen Elizabeth II knighted him in 1953. He presented the Mines and Quarries Act of 1954, improving the working environments for miners, and the Housing Repairs and Rent Act of 1955, which established housing standards.

These reforms became overshadowed by several foreign policies in Malaya and Kenya, where he then commanded military action. Even though successful over the rebellions, it was soon clear that they were no longer able to maintain their colonial rule.

With Winston's leadership and the help of the Allies, the British successfully held off Hitler. It was a brutal and long war.

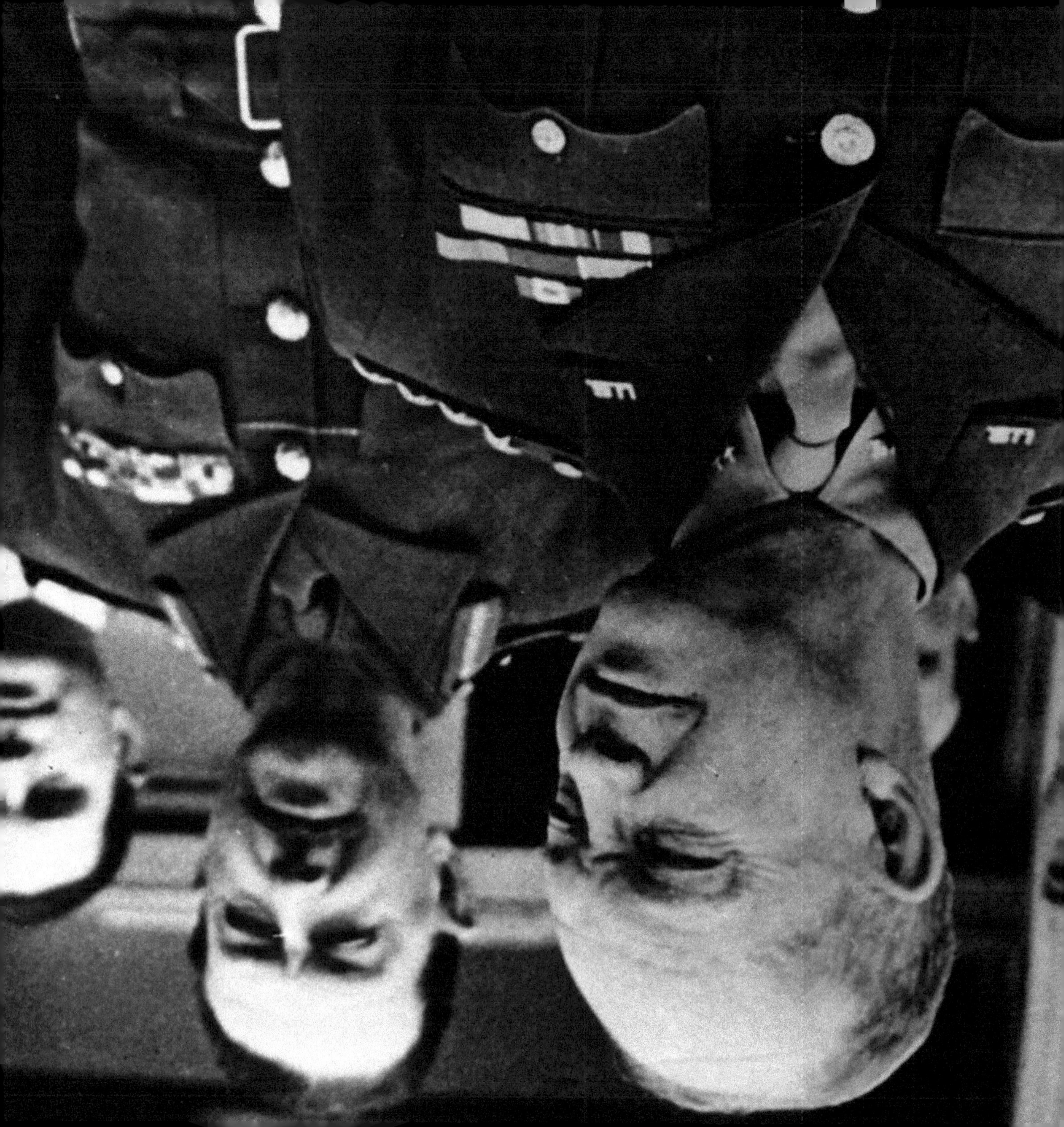

Sir Winston Churchill with Dwight D. Eisenhower

He became worried about the Soviet Union and the Red Army. He thought that they were as dangerous as Hitler and now the Germans had been defeated.

He was correct to be worried, and once World War II was over, the Cold War began between the Western nations of NATO (including USA, France, Britain) and the communist Soviet Union.

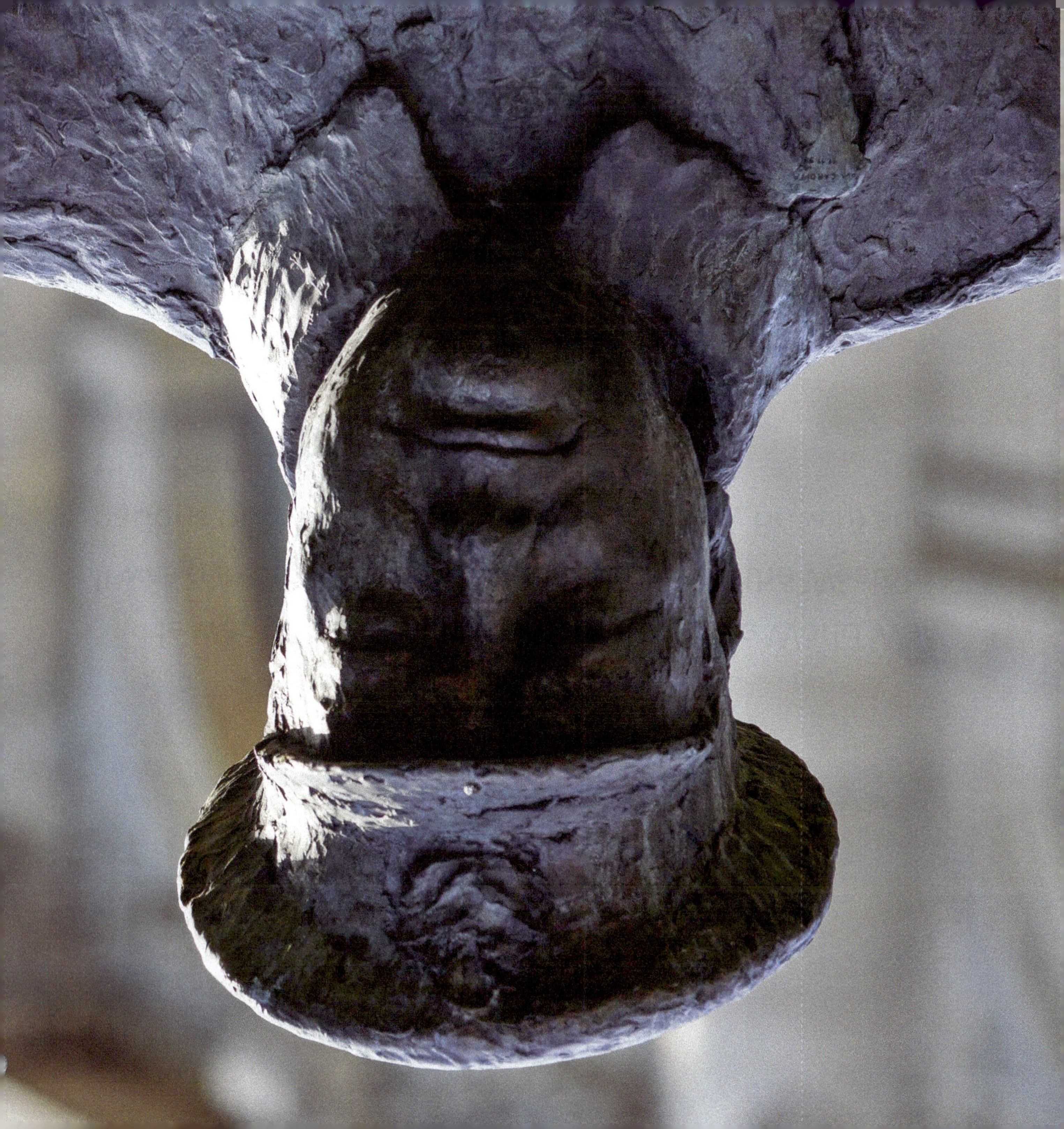

Sir Winston Churchill monument in Paris, France

LATER YEARS AND DEATH

He authored several historical books and in 1953 was awarded the Nobel Prize in Literature.

Churchill begin showing signs of failing health in 1941, when he visited the White House. He had a mild heart attack and had a similar attack in 1943, while suffering from pneumonia. At 78, in June 1953, he had a series of strokes while at his office.

They were able to keep the news from the Parliament and the public, with an announcement coming out stating he was only exhausted. He was able to recuperate at home and would return to work in October as Prime Minister.

Sir Winston Churchill with son and grandson

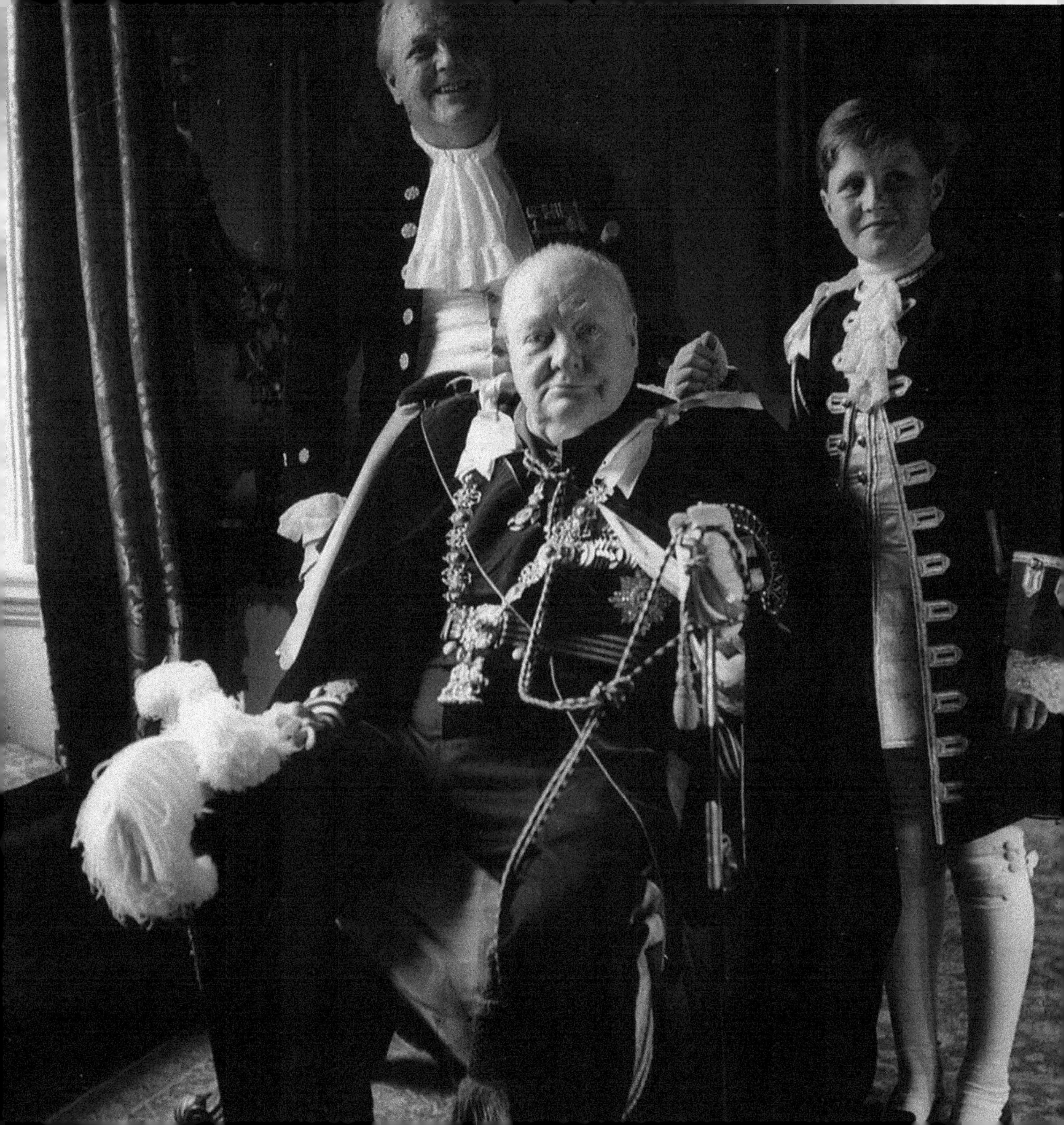

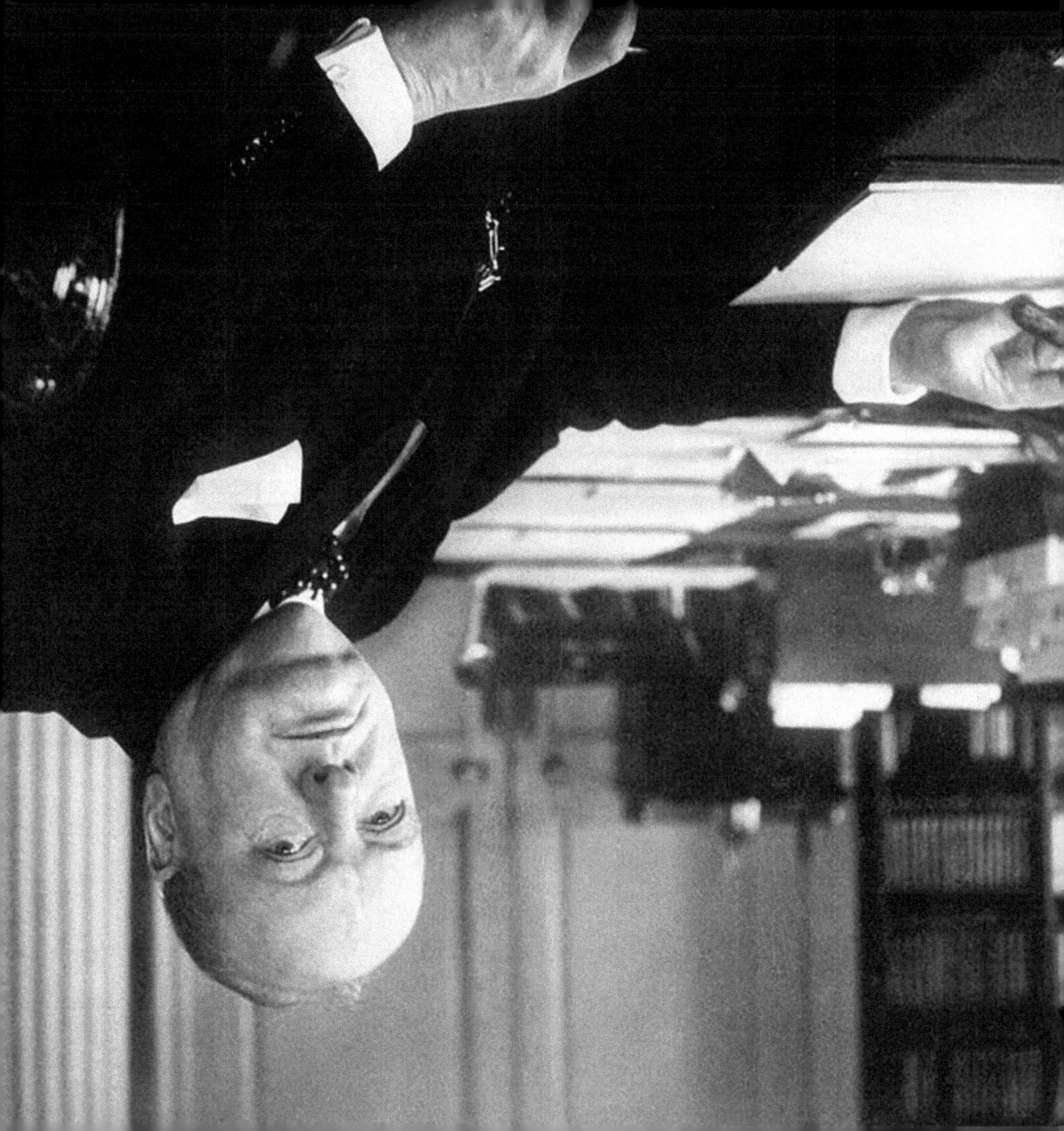

It became apparent, even to him, that he was now mentally and physically slowing down and he retired in 1955. He remained as a Parliament member until 1964 when he decided not to run for re-election in the general election.

Winston Churchill as Prime Minister 1940-1945

Some speculated that Churchill suffering from Alzheimer's disease during his final years, but several experts in the medical field felt that his symptoms were more a consequence of the strokes he had suffered earlier in his life. He continued to be active in public life, even though it was done from his homes in Kent and Hyde Park Gate, located in London.

Sir Winston Churchill with wife Clementine Churchill

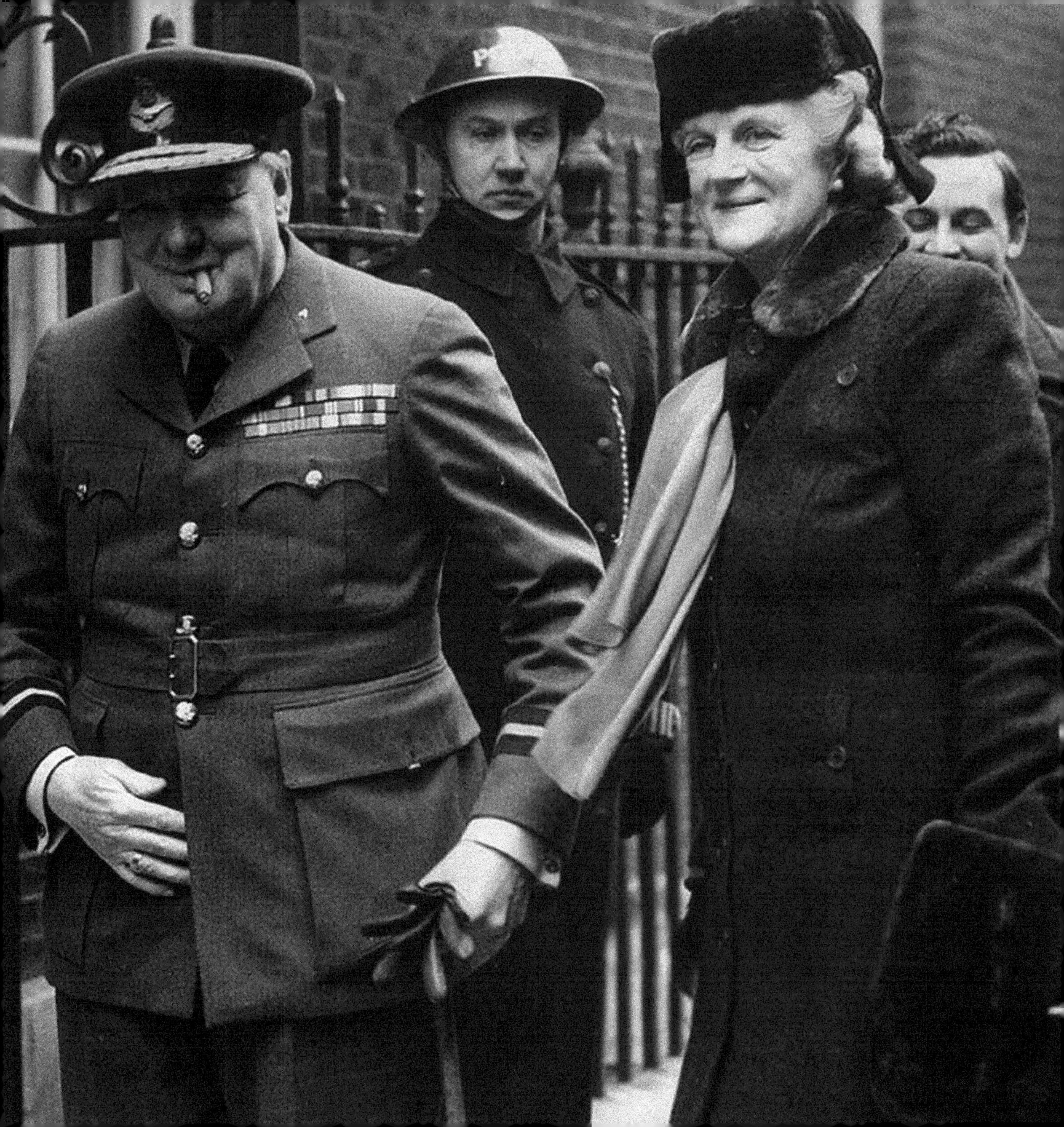
P

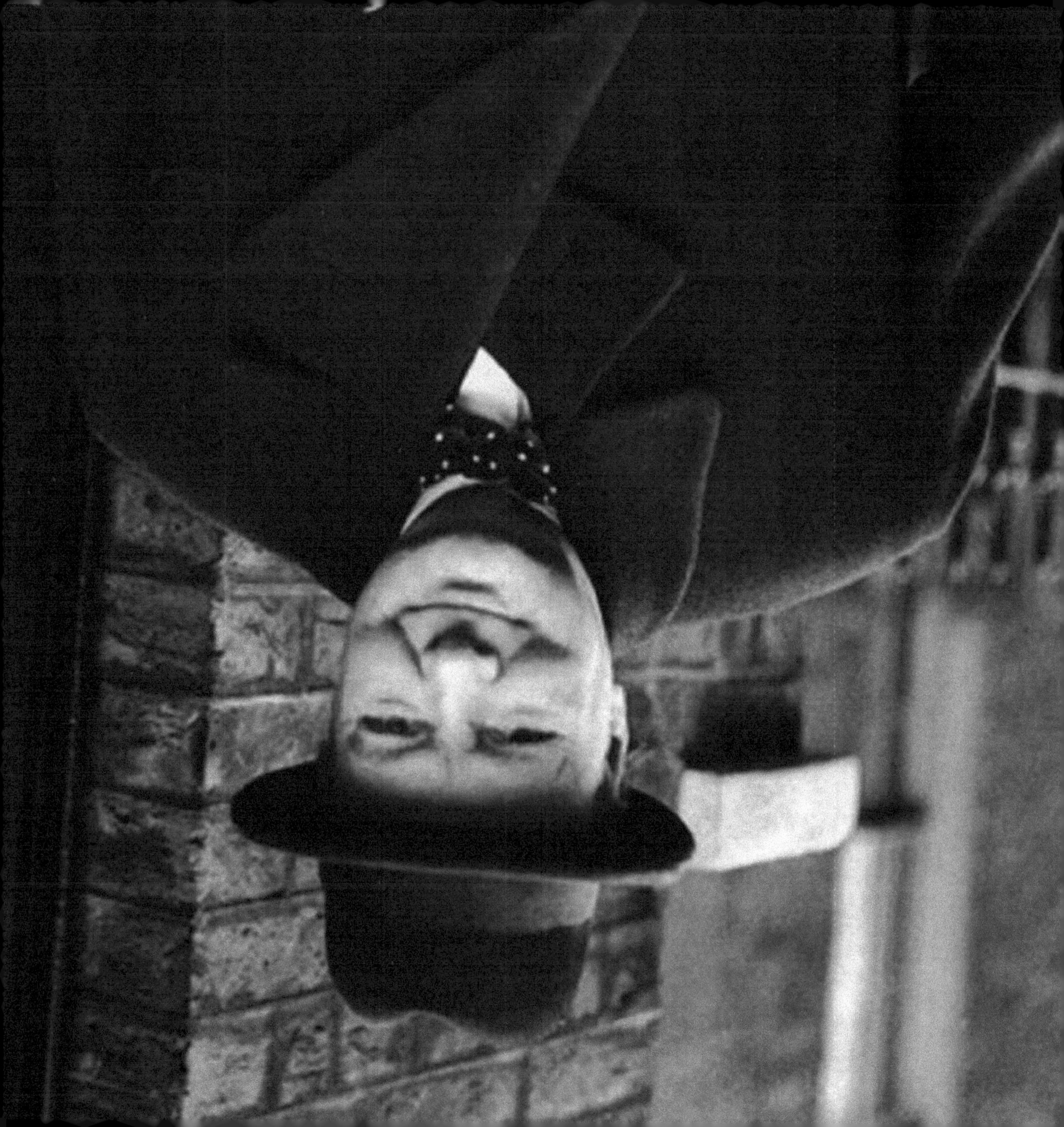

He then had a severe stroke on January 15, 1965, leaving him gravely ill. He then passed away nine days later at his London home, on January 24, 1965, at the age of 90. He was mourned by Britain for longer than a week.

Sir Winston Churchill with smiling

FAMOUS QUOTES

Winston was known for his rousing quotes and speeches. Below are some of his famous quotes:

In a speech where he criticized the appeasement of Hitler, he said *"You were given the choice between war and dishonor. You chose dishonor, and you will have war."*

Sir Winston Churchill in a jeep outside the German Reichstag during a tour of the ruined city of Berlin, 1945

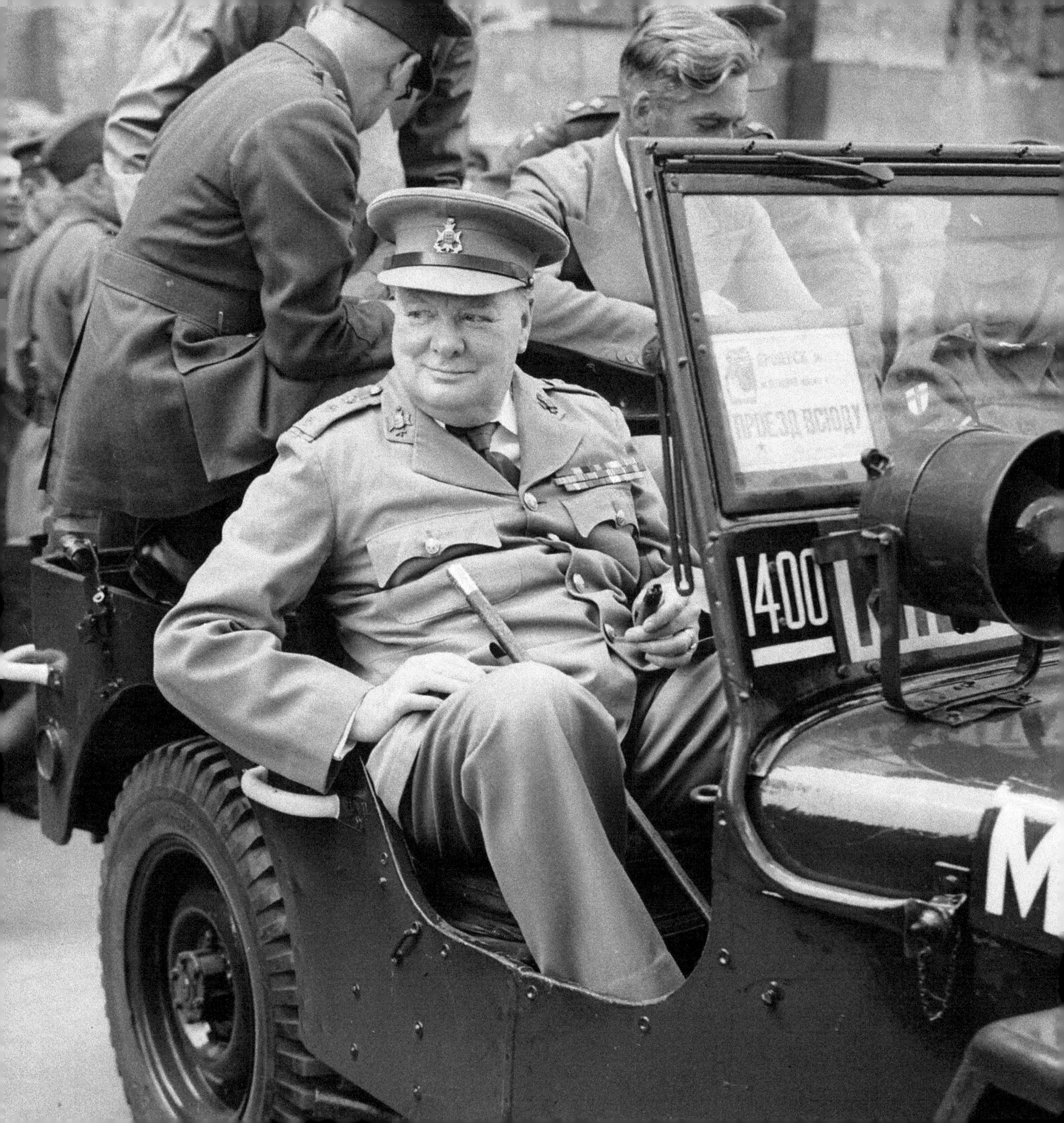
ПРОЕЗД ВСЮДУ
1400

*Sir Winston Churchill's coffin being lifted to the
Westminster Abbey by pallbearers*

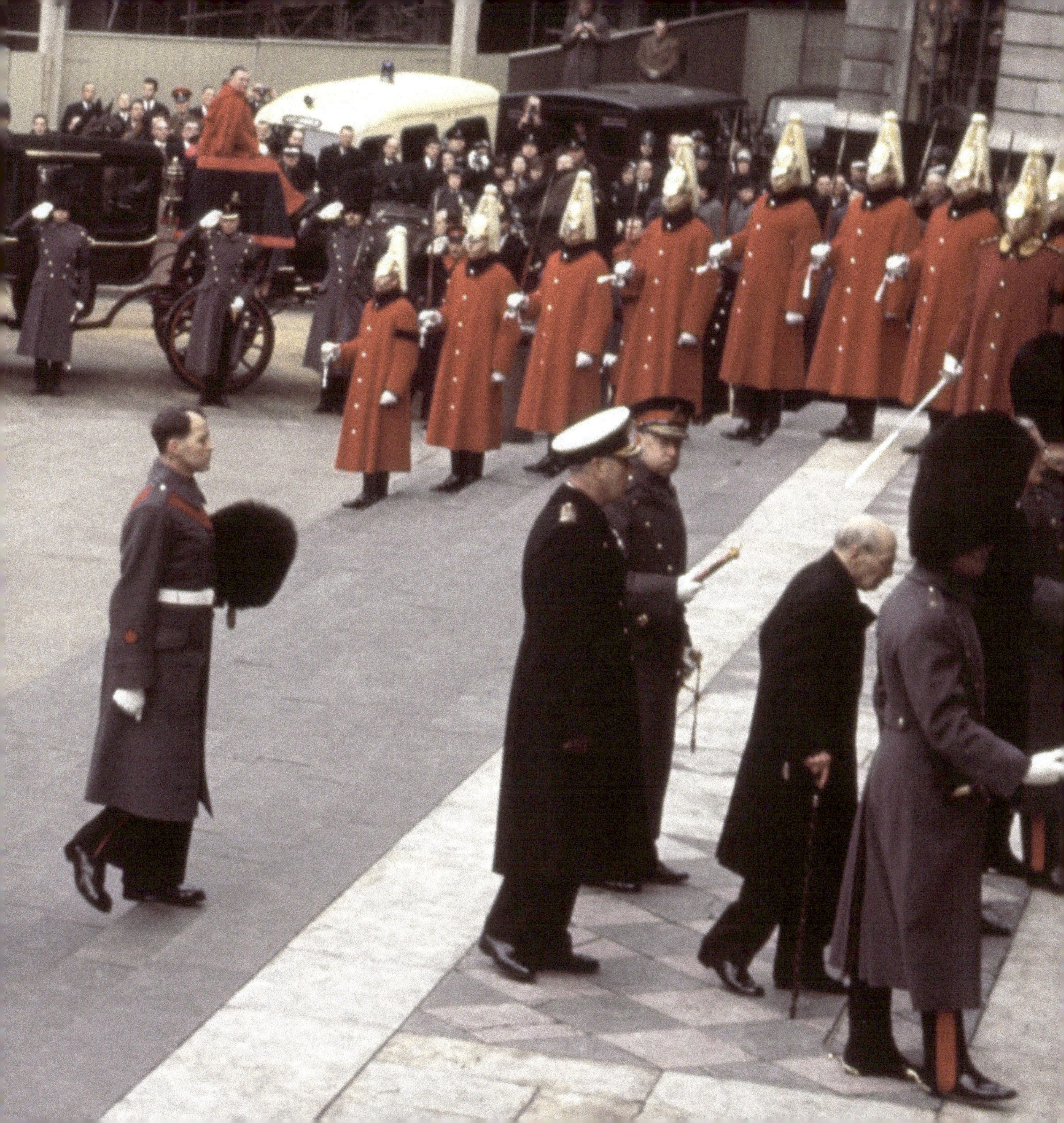

He also commented regarding the appeasement: *"An appeaser is one who feeds a crocodile, hoping it will eat him last."*

Sir Winston Churchill was a great leader who spent his life in service to his country.

For more quotes and additional information about Winston Churchill research the internet, go to your local library, and ask questions of your teachers, family, and friends.

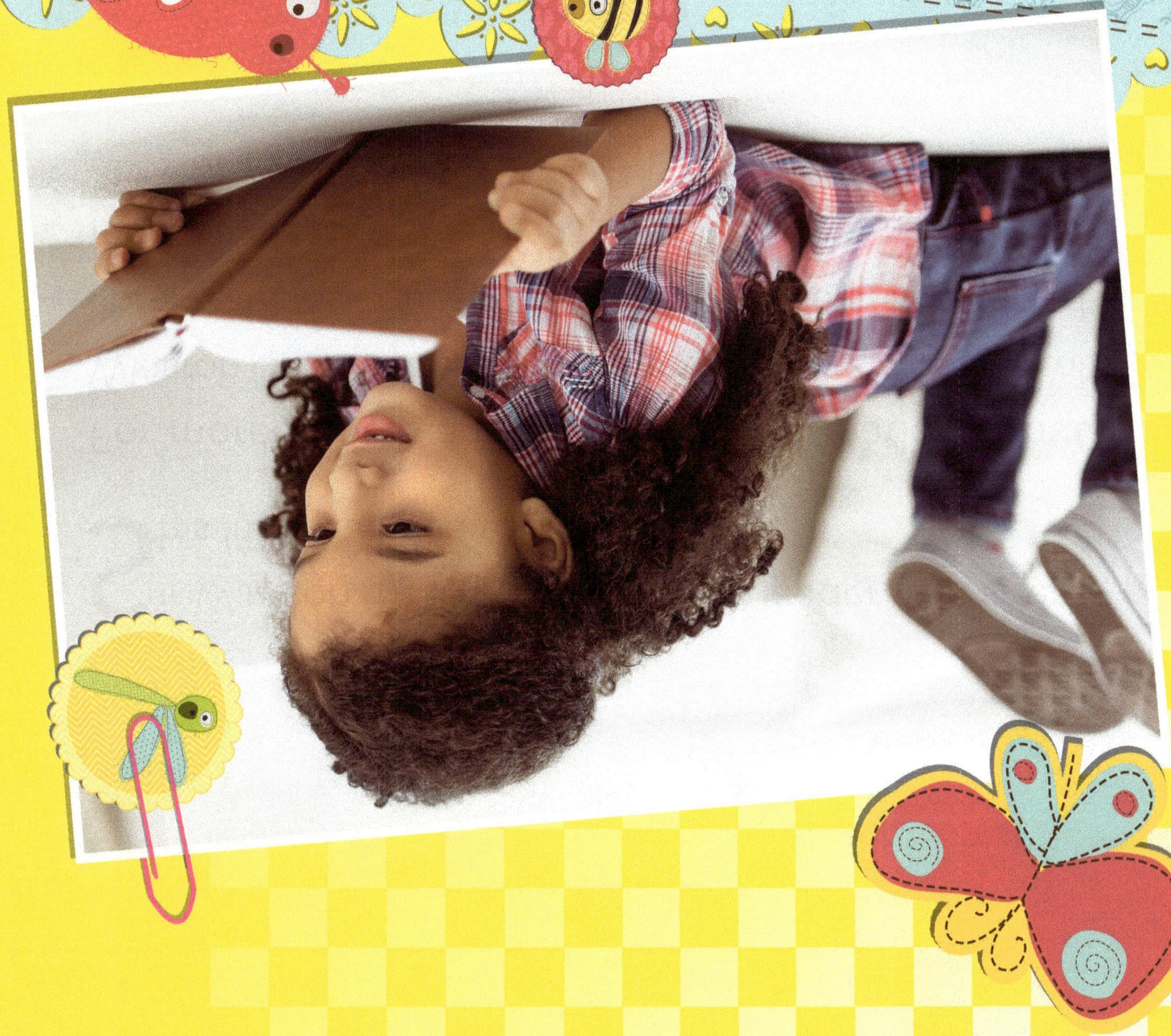

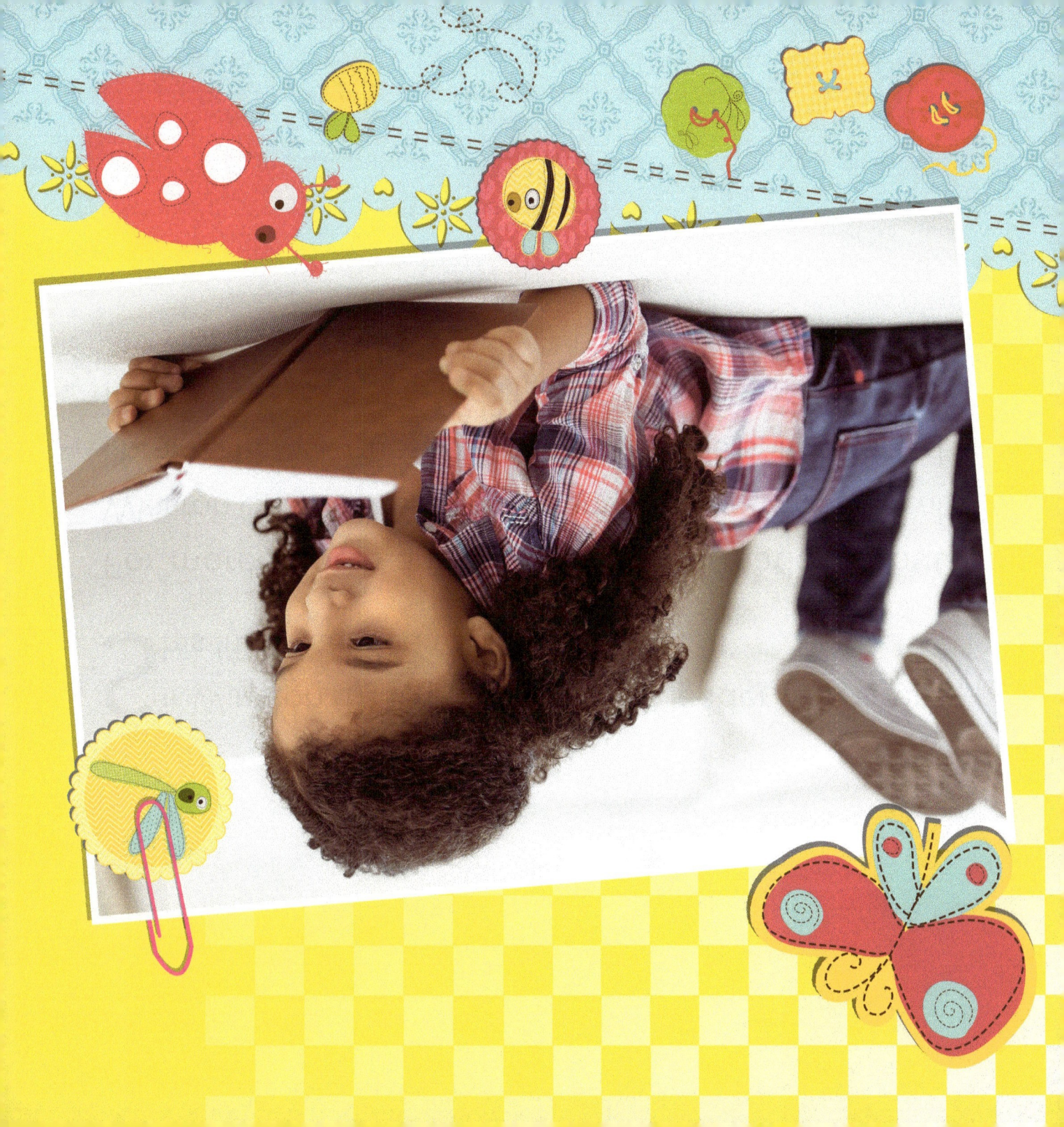

Visit

BABY PROFESSOR
EDUCATION KIDS

www.BabyProfessorBooks.com

to download Free Baby Professor eBooks and view our catalog of new and exciting Children's Books